real baby animals
mitzi, molly, and max the kittens

by Gisela Buck and Siegfried Buck

For a free color catalog describing Gareth Stevens' list of high-quality books, call 1-800-542-2595 (USA) or 1-800-461-9120 (Canada). Gareth Stevens' Fax: (414) 225-0377.

Library of Congress Cataloging-in-Publication Data available upon request from publisher. Fax: (414) 225-0377 for the attention of the Publishing Records Department.

ISBN 0-8368-1503-3

This North American edition first published in 1996 by
Gareth Stevens Publishing
1555 North RiverCenter Drive, Suite 201
Milwaukee, Wisconsin 53212 USA

This edition first published in 1996 by Gareth Stevens, Inc. Original edition © 1994 by Kinderbuchverlag KBV Luzern (Sauerländer, AG), Aarau, Switzerland, under the title *Lissi, Mira und Max, drei kleine Katzen*.

Translated from the German by John E. Hayes. Adapted by Gareth Stevens, Inc. All additional material supplied for this edition © 1996 by Gareth Stevens, Inc.

Photographer: Andreas Fischer-Nagel
Watercolor artist: Wolfgang Kill
Series editor: Patricia Lantier-Sampon
Editorial assistants: Diane Laska, Jamie Daniel

Printed in Mexico

1 2 3 4 5 6 7 8 9 99 98 97 96

Gareth Stevens Publishing
MILWAUKEE

Mitzi, Molly, and Max are five weeks old.

Their eyes are still blue, like all young

kittens' eyes.

Today, they are going into the backyard for the first time with their mother, Mascha.

Max sits with his mother.
Mitzi is curious and
walks off alone.
She tiptoes carefully
through the grass.

Molly watches everything
closely. She sees and hears
movements everywhere.

4

The kittens love to play together with Mascha.

They learn a lot from her.

The kittens practice how to pounce, catch, and prowl. They bite each other playfully and retract their claws when they fight.

The kittens must learn how to drink milk in a bowl. At first, they splash the milk all over themselves.

Later, they try eating some ground cat food along with their milk. Molly inspects it first with her paws. Max waits cautiously.

The kittens wash themselves after eating. They lick their paws and use them to wipe their faces, ears, and the backs of their heads. Then they lick their bodies clean with their tongues.

Molly is already taking her
afternoon nap. Her paws
move a lot when she sleeps.
Is she playing in her dreams?

Mitzi is tired, too.

She does not want
to be petted now.
That is why she hisses
at every intruder.

Max has to go to the bathroom. He looks for a dry spot in the garden. Then he scratches some dirt aside.

He squats carefully.

When he is finished, he covers up everything neatly.

The three kittens play again after their nap. Molly discovers a ball of red yarn.

Then they play hide-and-seek in the yellow watering can.

The kittens nurse, or drink their mother's milk, until they are eight weeks old. Then they will get most of their food from bowls.

Neighbors come to visit with their dachshund, Troll. They keep him on his leash for safety reasons.

Mitzi arches her back.
She tries to frighten Troll.

Molly is afraid. She runs away
and climbs on a branch. She
can't do this very well yet.

Max is frightened, too, and he hides in a tree.

Sometimes Mascha and her kittens
will stay outside at night. The
hedgehog at their feeding bowl
does not bother them.

Cats are nocturnal animals and can see well in the dark. The pupils of their eyes open very wide.

Their pupils close in bright light.

Molly has caught her first mouse. Cats are predatory animals.

They retract their claws when they prowl.

They push their claws out when they pounce.

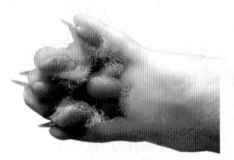

Mascha's kittens are independent
now; they can live apart from her.
David chooses Molly as his pet.
Molly will be happy with him.
Max and Mitzi will go with his
cousin, Isabella.

Further Reading and Videos

Animal Babies in the Wild. (Karl-Lorimar Video)
Animals At A Glance (4 volumes). (Gareth Stevens)
The Boy Who Drew Cats. (Rabbit Ears Video)
The Boy Who Drew Cats: A Japanese Folktale. A. Levine (Dial)
Cats. Norman Barrett (Watts)
Cats, Big and Little. Beatrice Fontanel (Young Discovery Library)
I Can Read About Cats and Kittens. George Wolff (Troll Associates)
The Kids' Cat Book. Tomie De Paola (Holiday)
Oscar, Cat-about-Town. James Herriot (St. Martin)
Our New Kitten. Harriet Hains (Dorling Kindersley)
The Tiger and the Brahmin. (Rabbit Ears Video)

Fun Facts about Cats and Kittens

Did you know . . .

— that the kittens we love as house pets are relatives of the huge
    tigers and lions in the zoo?
— that cats don't perspire when it is hot?
— that a typical house cat will shed over 90 pounds
    (40 kilograms) of fur in its lifetime?
— that cats and kittens make a lovely purring sound when they are
    happy or content?
— that cats use their whiskers to help judge how wide spaces are
    before they try to get into or through them?

Glossary-Index

arch (v) — to take on a curved shape (p. 17).

curious — eager to learn (p. 4).

intruder — someone or something that is unwelcome or threatening (p. 11).

leash — a chain or strap attached to a collar and used to hold or lead an animal from place to place (p. 16).

nap — a very short sleep (pp. 10, 13).

nocturnal — active during the night (p. 20).

nurse (v) — to drink the milk produced by a female mammal's body (p. 15).

pounce — to jump on something quickly and unexpectedly (pp. 6, 21).

predatory — surviving by preying on other animals. Although many pet cats never go outside to hunt prey, they practice their predatory skills by chasing balls or playing with yarn or cat toys. Some also catch mice indoors (p. 21).

prowl — to move quietly and sneakily, as if looking for prey on which to pounce (pp. 6, 21).

pupil — the opening in the center of the eye through which light enters (p. 20).

retract — to pull in or take back; cats and kittens can retract their claws when the claws aren't needed (pp. 6, 21).